T0043452

Be The Change
BE
KIND

BE THE CHANGE: BE KIND

Copyright © Marcus Sedgwick, 2022

Illustrations © Thomas Taylor, 2022

All rights reserved.

No part of this book may be reproduced by any means, nor transmitted, nor translated into a machine language, without the written permission of the publishers.

Marcus Sedgwick has asserted his right to be identified as the author of this work in accordance with sections 77 and 78 of the Copyright, Designs and Patents Act 1988.

Condition of Sale
This book is sold subject to the condition that it shall not, by way of trade or otherwise, be lent, resold, hired out or otherwise circulated in any form of binding or cover other than that in which it is published and without a similar condition including this condition being imposed on the subsequent purchaser.

An Hachette UK Company
www.hachette.co.uk

Vie Books, an imprint of Summersdale Publishers Ltd
Part of Octopus Publishing Group Limited
Carmelite House
50 Victoria Embankment
LONDON
EC4Y 0DZ
UK

www.summersdale.com

Printed and bound in China

ISBN: 978-1-80007-411-8

Substantial discounts on bulk quantities of Summersdale books are available to corporations, professional associations and other organizations. For details contact general enquiries: telephone: +44 (0) 1243 771107 or email: enquiries@summersdale.com.

Be The Change
BE KIND
Rise Up and Make a Difference to The World
MARCUS SEDGWICK
illustrated by THOMAS TAYLOR
vie

CONTENTS

Introduction

My name is Marcus Sedgwick and over the last 20 years or so I've written a lot of books for young people. After a few years of this, someone pointed out that my books often tended to have protagonists who were kind and decent people, but who found themselves in difficult situations. That started me thinking about why I had felt drawn to do that (because it wasn't then a conscious choice) and it didn't take Sigmund Freud to figure out why. I also started to study kindness; what we mean by it, where it comes from and so on. Put simply, this book you now hold in your hands is the book I wish I had had when I was young. That's because I found the other kids around me at school, and even the teachers sometimes, to often be very cynical and unkind, even cruel. This was the eighties, the era when selfishness was turned into a good thing; when slogans like "greed is good" were born, and when we were being told on all sides to "look out for number one" and "nice guys finish last". I often tried to argue with my friends that there was a better way, but I didn't know how; I didn't have the tools.

This book, I hope, is that tool.

How to use this book

This book is for you. You're a nice person. I know that you are. How do I know that? For one thing, because you've picked up a book about kindness, and you already want to know more. Secondly, because, as we'll see later, kindness is built into all of us, from before we're even born. You might already be thinking of people you know who don't seem so nice, but that's almost always because they are reacting to bad things that have happened in their life. And how do we get past the bad things that happen in life? Well, one really important way is with understanding and love. In a single word, with kindness!

So, this is a book that will show you why kindness is so important and how to argue that point with anyone who's not so convinced.

It's a simple book about a deceptively complex subject and I hope you're going to find the subject as fascinating as I do.

It's best to read it from the beginning to the end, as we're going to be following a story of kinds. But, of course, you can always go back and reread any sections that were hard to understand the first time around, or any bits that you want to really remember.

So, read on and have fun!

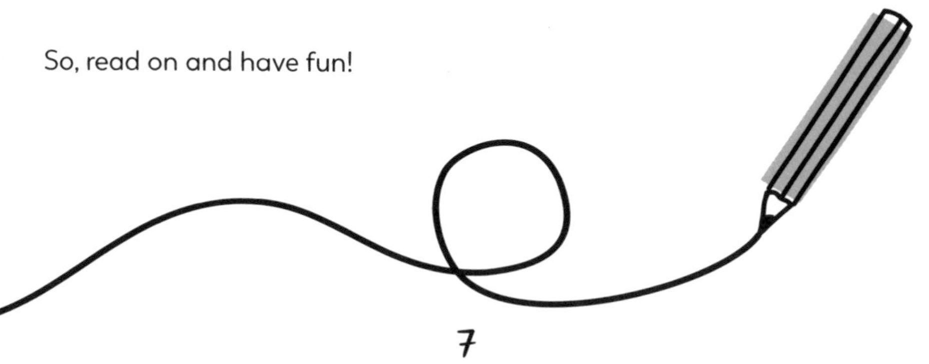

Chapter 1

What is kindness?

It might sound silly to ask: everyone knows what kindness is, right? But one of the things we'll see is that the apparently simple concept of kindness becomes complicated very quickly. So, in this chapter we're going to take a proper look.

What do we even mean by kindness?

It's such an everyday notion that maybe we never stop to think what it means, *exactly*. But since this whole book is about it, we ought to know what we're talking about.

Why don't you write down what you think kindness is? Do it right here, before we go any further:

Did you find that easy?

Now, let's see what the dictionary says, and see if it's anything like what you've written!

> Kindness – the quality of being disposed to do good to others.

This is a bit of a mouthful, but that's why words exist – so we have one word and not a whole sentence to say something we all understand.

Or *think* we understand, at least, because one of the things we're going to discover in this book is that the question of kindness is much more complicated than we might think.

Before we go on, here's another question for you, and it's a big one...

HOW KIND ARE YOU?

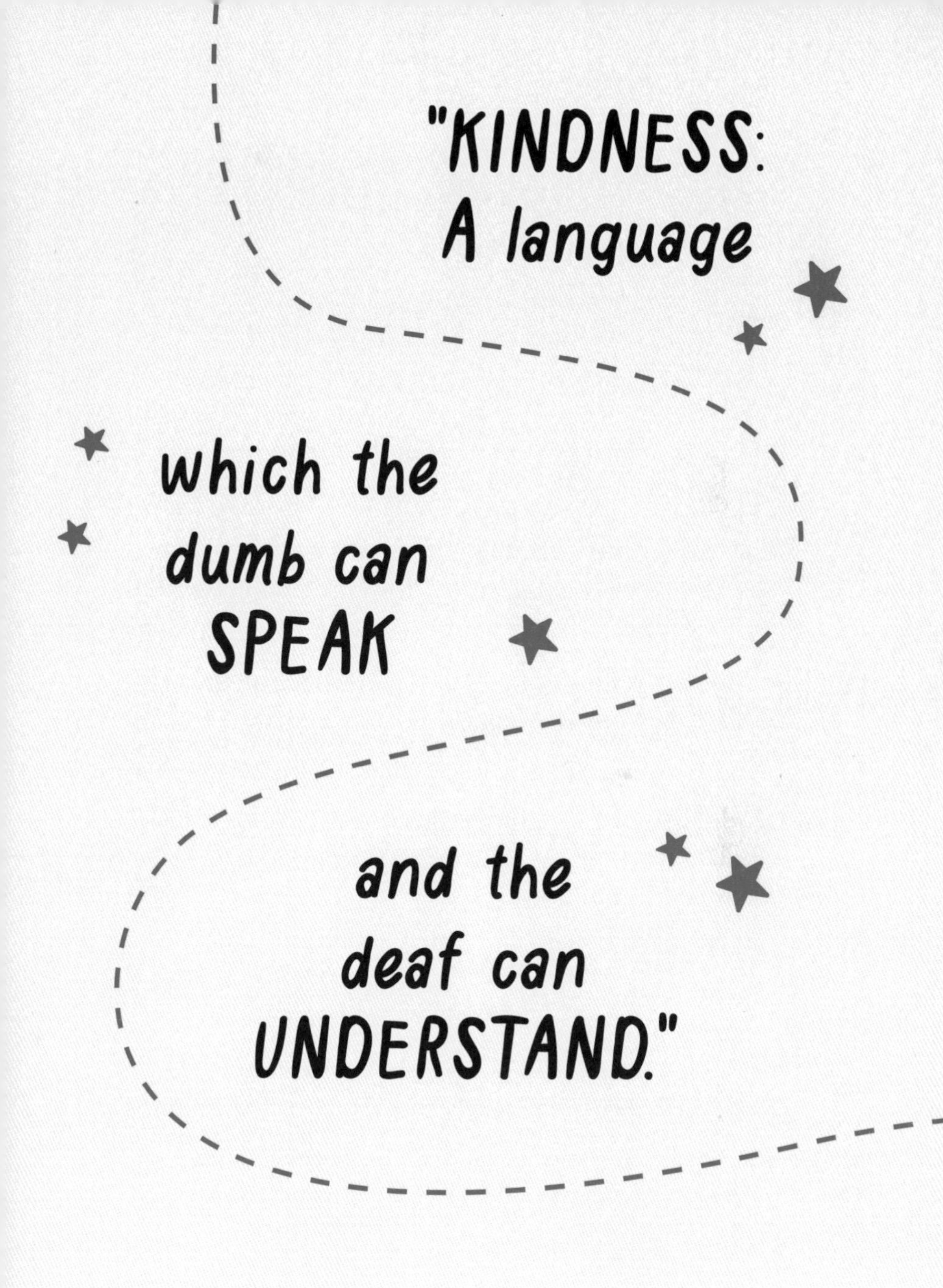

Christian Nestell Bovee

How do you feel about kindness?

1. It's really important. The world needs as much of it as possible.

2. It's a nice idea in principle and everyone should try to be kind but you have to look after yourself first and foremost.

3. What's the point? Everyone is basically selfish, so it makes sense to be selfish too. It's a "dog-eat-dog world"*.

4. Or maybe you have some other opinion? This is a big subject after all!

*You might have heard people use this expression. It means they think that people behave the way wild animals do; i.e. if you don't eat "the other dog", the "other dog" will eat you. We'll look at this more later, because people who think this might just have the wrong idea about the animal kingdom.

If so, write it in here (or even sketch it!):

Have a think about yourself

Do you often act with kindness towards others? Who does your kindness extend to? Which one of the below best describes you? If none of them do, write in what you feel about yourself at the end.

1. **I am kind to everyone, as much as I possibly can be anyway: family, friends and strangers.**
2. **I try to be kind, and although I'm not an angel, I'm generally kind to my family and friends. But strangers? Not so much.**
3. **I don't see why I should be kind to people. But if they do something good for me, then I might help them another time.**
4. **I don't bother with kindness. It's a waste of time; it's only for losers. The world is tough and the sooner you get used to that the better.**
5. **Or, try to write a description of your own attitude to kindness here...**

Great! Now we have some idea of what kindness is, and how you feel about it.

Chapter 2
What would you do?

In this chapter it's time to get our hands dirty! We're going to imagine ourselves right into the question of what it means to be kind.

Put yourself in this scene:

It's Saturday afternoon. You've just strolled to the supermarket to grab some snacks to munch while you watch TV later. You're not thinking about very much apart from crisps, but in the next few minutes, three different, unexpected situations will arise.

How do you react to each one?

Situation One – The mother
You're leaving the shop, carrying a small bag of groceries. A mother is heading for the doors, with two bags of shopping in her arms and a wailing toddler in tow. You can make her day a little better by holding the door open for her so she can get outside more easily.

But here's another situation:

And finally, this situation might just happen instead:

Situation Three – The kid

Finally, you're making your way across the car park. It's on a steep slope and you're trudging uphill. People are getting in and out of their cars, loading shopping, stowing kids in car seats.

You're approaching a truck when it starts moving. Suddenly, you realize it's not under control; there's no driver in the cab, and it's rolling backward, downhill, towards a car, where a small boy is waiting for his dad to return a shopping trolley.

The boy hasn't seen the truck; he's going to be killed. Without even having to work it out, you know his only chance is for you to leap over and push him out of the way. There's no time to think, but you'd definitely be putting your own life at risk.

So, what do you think you would do in each situation?

Do you hold the door for the mother with the shopping bags?

Do you help the old man pick up his dropped shopping?

And finally, the big one, do you leap in front of the car to save the boy's life? Do you risk your life to save someone else's? And a complete stranger's, at that.

Three situations:

- **one very mild,**
- **one a little troublesome,**
- **and one life-threatening.**

Each situation is crying out for an act of kindness from someone; but the first is very small, while the last is *very* big. Perhaps the biggest act of kindness of all we can imagine.

What were your responses?

Perhaps you thought: of course, I'd hold the door for the mother.

Maybe I'd help the old man if it was raining, or no one else looked like they were going to.

As for the kid about to be crushed; well, I'd like to think I would, of course, but honestly, who knows until something like that happens to them?

Those are good answers, ones that many people would give, but not everyone. Some people might not even care to help the old man or the mother, never mind risk their lives to save someone else's. But these are all acts of kindness. The first two are about everyday acts of kindness; the third one is, fortunately, an example of a very rare kind of scenario. But such things do happen.

Random acts of kindness

In 1886, in Dunfermline, Scotland, 17-year-old William Hunter threw himself into the town loch in an attempt to save the life of 15-year-old Andrew Robson, who had got into difficulties while swimming in the cold water. Despite William's effort, however, both drowned.

The drowning of William and Andrew so moved the famous businessman Andrew Carnegie that he donated money to honour William Hunter with a memorial.

Coming from a humble background, Carnegie was a Scotsman who moved to the US and became the richest man in the world. He was a philanthropist* who, among other things, built hundreds of libraries so that the poor could educate themselves, just as he had been able to. (You may have read books at school that were competing to win the Carnegie Medal, which is named after Andrew Carnegie.)

Later, he established an organization to celebrate and reward those performing selfless acts of courage to help others in danger. The Carnegie Hero Fund Trust is still going strong today, with branches in the USA, the UK and various European countries.

*** A philanthropist is someone who does good things for other people. The word derives from two Greek words meaning "love" and "man", and can refer to any kind of good deed. However, these days the word is most commonly used to refer to rich people making donations of money to worthwhile causes.**

Everyday superheroes

A heroic act of self-sacrifice is possibly the ultimate example of kindness. We'll look at more examples of that nature later, but one really important message of this book is that you don't have to be a superhero to be kind: it's just as important to act with kindness on a day-to-day basis.

Isn't it?

I would say it is, but not everyone would. Even if you agree with the view that everyday kindness makes the world a better place, not everyone would have the same explanation for why they would do what they said they would, from holding the door open for the mother, to leaping to save the small boy.

What seems to be such a simple concept, kindness, gets more complicated the more you look at it. Arguments have raged for centuries about kindness, about what it is, and whether we should be kind. About why we behave the way we do. Some of the greatest minds of all time have really struggled to explain things such as why we might risk our lives to save a stranger's.

Other people even question whether kindness exists, despite examples of all kinds from everyday life that appear to show it in action.

Kindness is everywhere

Let's do a quick exercise to prove that there is more kindness in the world than we might at first think. We very often overlook the little things in life, so take the left-hand side of the next page to jot down as many examples from your own life, either recently or long ago, where people have done kind things for you. Then, on the right, where you have done kind things for other people. You might have done some very big things, but here we really just want to notice all the little things you do for people too, from telling your friend that their new bag is cool, to helping your mum or dad carry the shopping in from the car.

So, you've thought about your own acts of kindness, and you're probably a very kind person, but we still have the big questions to consider, such as:

- **What *is* kindness?**
- **Why and how does it exist?**
- **Lastly, and perhaps most importantly of all: why should we be good towards other people?**

To answer these questions, we're going to take a brief walk through a few thousand years of human history. It's a long, long journey that I'm going to shorten and simplify.

Along the way we'll come across some brilliant ideas and some crazy ones. We'll see geniuses trapped by the logic of their own theories. We'll see people die for their beliefs. We'll even come face to face with the extinction of human life on Earth!

Chapter 3

Where does kindness come from?

So where did kindness begin? Well, it's been around a long time and another thing that's been around a long time is RELIGION.

So what does religion have to say about kindness? Basically, it's this:

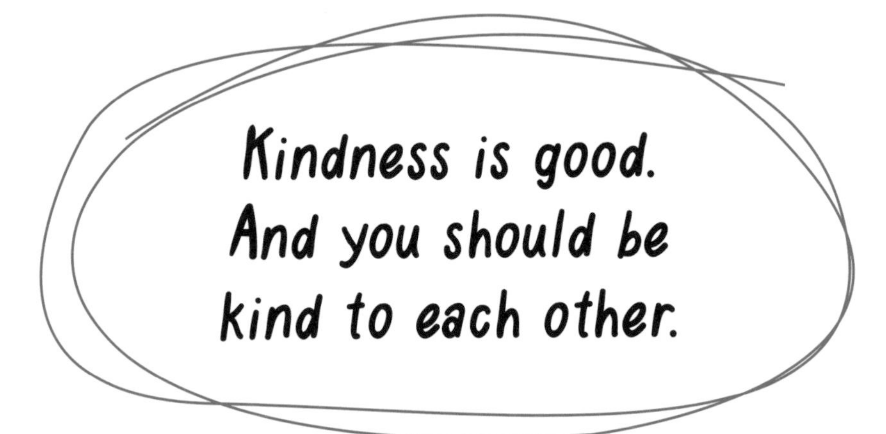

And here endeth the chapter about religion.

You might be thinking, *wait!* That's all there is to be said about religion?

Well, of course there's much more to say, but this is the thing about religion; if you have a religious faith of some kind, you're meant to do what that religion tells you is the right thing to do. The world's five major religions, which are to say Christianity, Islam, Hinduism, Buddhism and Judaism, all have some instructions in their holy texts that tell us we ought to be kind.

We could spend a long time digging into this further, but really, if you believe in God, you're supposed to be good; it doesn't really matter what you think, *those are the rules.*

So, what if you do believe in a god, but have trouble behaving in the way your holy book tells you to? Does it take a god to tell us to be good? What if you don't believe in a god of any kind? How else might you decide that it's good to be kind?

Reasons to be kind

Can you work out a good reason to be kind without a god or a holy book, such as the Bible or the Koran, to tell you to?

Well, think on these points:

1. **A little imagination tells us that if we find something that's done to us to be good, then we can assume that others will find it good too.**
2. **On the other hand, it's not hard to imagine that if we find something that's done to us to be unpleasant, then so would others.**
3. **From here it is a very short step to conclude that we might avoid a lot of problems for everyone if we stick to one simple rule...**

"DO TO OTHERS AS YOU WOULD WANT THEM DO TO YOU."

There's a couple of things to say about this rule. First, I didn't just make it up. You probably worked it out for yourself when you were in pre-school. In fact, lots of people have worked it out, across the centuries, in many different cultures. It's called: the golden rule.

Actually, the simple idea of kindness can get very confusing, as we will see when we enter the wonderfully weird world of PHILOSOPHY!

"There is no religion
without love,

and people may talk
as much as they like
about their religion,

but if it does not teach them to be good and kind to man and beast,

it is all a sham..."

from *Black Beauty*, by Anna Sewell, a book which changed people's attitudes towards kindness to animals.

Philosophy – or, the theory of everything!

Given that it's the study of fundamental ideas about life, philosophy is a HUGE subject, and it's not surprising that philosophers have had a lot to say about kindness over the centuries. In this chapter, we're going to look at what they've said*.

"Do to others as you would have them do to you."

Isn't the golden rule enough? If everyone lived by that rule, wouldn't the world be wonderful?

We didn't say much about religion in the previous section, and maybe that was unfair, because the golden rule does first appear in a religious

context. Just not perhaps the one you're expecting. Although in the Bible Jesus said, "Do unto others as you would have them do unto you", the first known version we have of the rule is around 2,000 years older! It comes from Ancient Egypt, where the wisdom of Ma'at, the goddess of truth, morality and harmony is recounted in a story called *The Eloquent Peasant.*

*** We ought to remember before we go on, that, thousands of years ago, there wasn't much separation between philosophy and religion.**

"Do for one who may do for you; that you may cause him thus to do."

That sounds a bit odd, but what it's basically saying is you should consider your actions towards someone else because it will affect how they behave towards you.

This is considered to be the first recorded example of any form of the golden rule, and it's 4,000 years old.

Sometime later, in Ancient Rome, we find something similar captured in a much shorter form: *do ut des* – which roughly translates from Latin as "I give that you might give".

This still isn't exactly what we mean by the golden rule either, but it's close.

In this, and the Ancient Egyptian version, there's the idea that your actions affect someone else's actions, and vice versa. It's a very short step from there to the golden rule itself, which appears again and again in the ancient world, in Greece, India, Persia and so on, in various forms.

For example, in Mahābhārata, the ancient Sanskrit epic of India, we find this:

> ***"One should never do something to others that one would regard as an injury to one's own self."***

In the Tamil tradition, in the Book of Virtue, we find this:

"Do not do to others what you know has hurt yourself."

In Ancient Persia, in the Pahlavi Texts, we have this:

"Whatever is disagreeable to yourself do not do unto others."

While in China, 500 years before Jesus, the legendary philosopher Confucius said:

"Do not impose on others what you do not wish for yourself."

The list could go on...

Here are three Greek philosophers:

Thales:

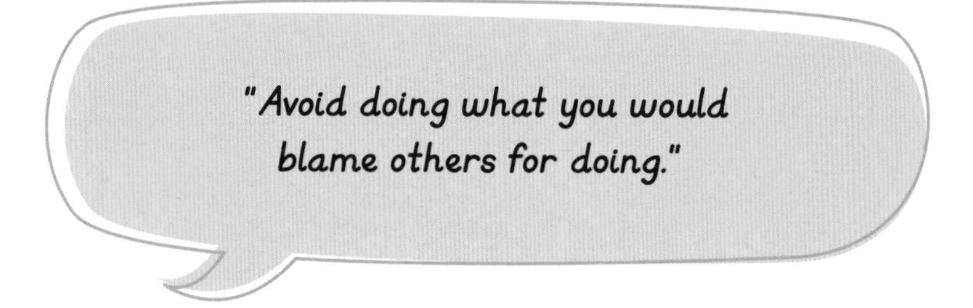

Epictetus:

"What you avoid suffering, do not attempt to make others suffer."

And here's the legendary Aristotle, who lived between 384 and 322 BCE:

"As the virtuous man is to himself, he is to his friend also, for his friend is another self."

Although the idea had been floating around for millions of years, it started to be called "the golden rule" explicitly by a few English theologians* in the early seventeenth century, such as Edward Topsell (who's most famous for his bestiaries, or books about animals) and Charles Gibbon, who wrote in 1604:

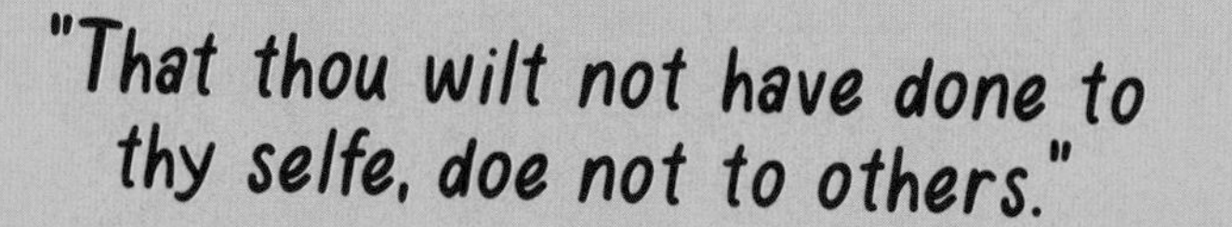

Let's put that into easier, modern English, and turn it from a negative statement into a positive one:

*** In general terms, theologians are people who study religious matters.**

So isn't that enough?

Doesn't the golden rule tell us that it's good to be kind? Aren't we finished?

Well that's a very good question. Let's read on a little further...

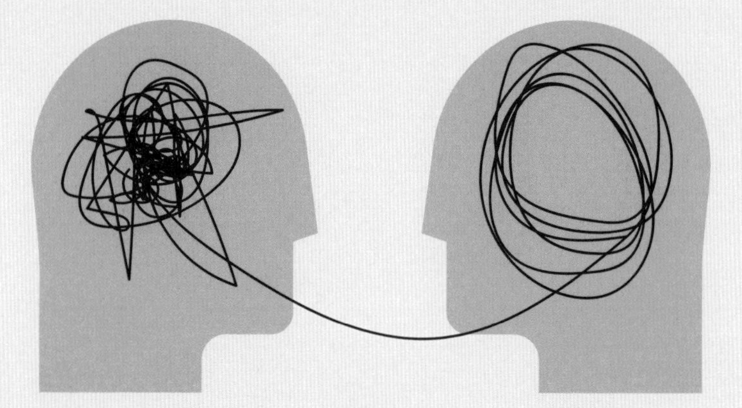

For one thing, the golden rule makes a lot of ASSUMPTIONS. It assumes that people have the imagination to understand what other people are feeling, something known as EMPATHY.

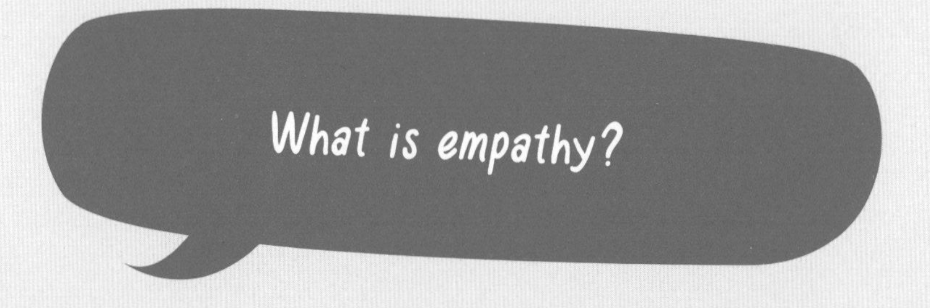

Empathy comes from two Greek words meaning "in" and "feeling", and describes the ability to use your imagination to enter into another person's world; to feel and experience things the way they do.

In their shoes

According to child psychologists (these are people who look at how children think, not children who are psychologists!), when we are very young, we don't really understand that we, and the rest of the world, are two different things. Then, at some point that varies from person to person; we begin to have a sense that we are one thing, and that other people and the world in general are separate from us. This can come as quite a shock! In fact, the "father" of psychoanalysis, Sigmund Freud, made the claim that this is the origin of most of our troubles – that we are always longing to return to this state of "oneness" with the world that we felt as young children.

Now, all that being said, because we are human, we are still able to understand how other people are feeling. Have a look at the situations on the following pages and write in the box beside each one how you think the person is feeling.

Ha
Ha
he he he
heh!

1

How did you find that? You probably had very little trouble in identifying how each of these people were feeling – and that's you using your empathy!

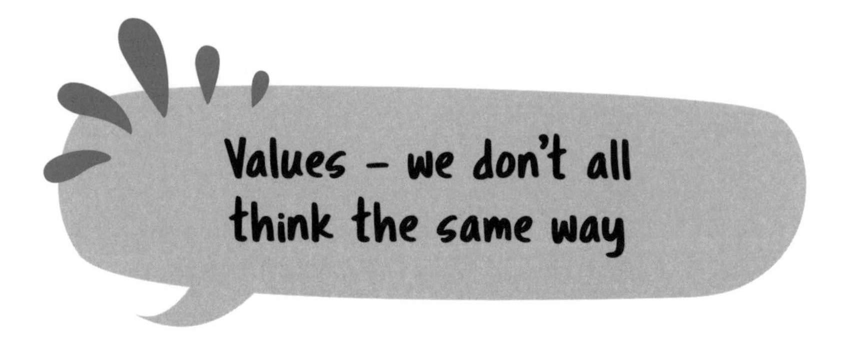

Values – we don't all think the same way

The golden rule assumes that we all want and value the same things, but what if what we want just *isn't the same* as what other people want?

It also assumes that everyone wants a situation that is best for everyone. Just because you and I might think that's desirable, we can't assume *everyone* does.

To be blunt: what if you just don't care about other people? What if you don't agree that life has to be fair to everyone? Who said it should be, after all? What if you think life is about looking after yourself, and getting what you want, however you can?

To makes things simple, suppose we were to divide the world into two types of people:

First, there are those who think we should act for the good of others (which may or may not include ourselves), and second, there are those who believe we should act for the good of ourselves.

If we go back to the golden rule and put each of these two types of people into it, we get the following results:

1. **For the first type, if you want other people to behave with kindness towards you, then you should behave with kindness towards other people.**
2. **For the second type, if you think that someone else shouldn't be expected to behave with kindness towards you, then why should you behave with kindness towards anyone else?**

All this means is that the golden rule can only get us to be kind if we are *already* kind. It's what we call a circular argument – because we're saying we are only kind because we're kind – that takes us back to where we started, like going round in a circle.

So, although the golden rule seems to get us as far as doing no harm to other people, doing nothing to them that they wouldn't want, it doesn't seem to get us as far as seeing why we should be kind to other people.

To go deeper, we're going to have to dig into a branch of philosophy known as ETHICS.

Philosophy is a vast subject that looks at all the different areas of human life; things such as existence, reality, knowledge, etc. One part of philosophy is called "ethics", and it's the area of thinking that examines how we should behave and looks at what good and bad are.

Ethics – the question of how we should behave

Ethics is a branch of philosophy that goes all the way back to the Ancient Greeks. It's about how people ought to behave and one of its most fundamental questions is this:

Are people basically good, or are they basically bad?

One of the most famous of all Greek philosophers was Socrates, who lived from roughly 470 to 399 BCE.

Socrates said, "The unexamined life is not worth living"; like many other Greek philosophers, he believed it was vital to "know thyself".

He also thought that when people really understood themselves, they would know what was right. Once they truly knew what was right, they would never do wrong.

This is an optimistic view of human nature: it argues that people only do bad things because they are mistaken, or cannot see what is real.

Was Socrates right? When we all know ourselves properly, will people stop doing bad things, and only do what's good?

Socrates

Moral relativism – what is "good", anyway?

One problem with Socrates' argument is that we've still said nothing here about what "good", or "right", actually are.

What if what I think is right, you think is *wrong*? What if we all hold different views about good and bad?

Who defines such things? God? Anyway, as we asked earlier, what if you don't believe in God?

This idea – the idea that there are no absolute "facts" or "truths" about what is good or what is bad, that it's just a question of what we all believe, *relative* to each other – is called MORAL RELATIVISM.

Now if you compare this idea with a subject like Maths, it's easy to see the difference – nothing is "relative" in Maths – a sum such as 36 + 24 has only one right answer, 60. No discussion, no debate, no grey areas.

Fact or feeling!?

Have a look at these examples – can you decide which are facts and which are just feelings or people's opinions?

Some of those were easy, some harder...

What's most interesting is this: *why* did you say what you said?

Right or wrong?

Socrates had lots of pupils, and one of them became another famous philosopher: Plato. Plato believed that the ideas of "right" and "wrong", "good" and "bad" were in fact as absolute as the truths in mathematics, such as 2 + 3 = 5. He believed that it was the task of philosophers to work out what these things were. (He also believed that this would be a very hard thing to do.)

Plato in turn had pupils, and one of them we have already met: Aristotle. He didn't buy his teacher's arguments about absolute truths, but we've already seen that he was a believer in the golden rule: Do to others as you would have them do to you.

He believed that one should start with the beliefs of ordinary people, look at what they *believe* to be good, and work from there. In that way, he believed, one could derive a system of good behaviour: ethics.

However, there's a problem with this argument: just as with trying to derive active kindness from the golden rule, it's a circular argument. Who are these "ordinary" people, anyway? Why should we think they're right about what "good" and "bad" are?

Altruism

Before we go further, we need to look at a special concept: altruism. Altruism is a fancy word but to many people it's simply another word for kindness. Others use it when they are speaking in special circumstances, in academic discussions, for example.

We ought to know exactly what it means but that's a problem, not everyone agrees.

The word was invented by a French philosopher, Auguste Comte, in the nineteenth century, and it derives from the Italian word for "others" – *altri* – so we know that our treatment of other people is central. Some people say there's another element which is vital in setting altruism apart from kindness, and that's this: there has to be some kind of COST to the person being kind for it to really be altruism. By "cost" we don't necessarily mean a cost in terms of money, but just something negative to the altruistic person; an extreme example would be putting our life in danger to save someone else. That risk is a cost, a pretty big one!

So what's the difference between kindness and altruism? To help illustrate this, think of these two examples.

In the first case, you're sitting on the bus home with a friend who missed what homework you're supposed to be doing. As you're kind, you explain what needs to be done, so they don't get into trouble.

In the second one, your friend has lost their copy of the book you both need to do your homework. Even though you need it too, you lend it to your friend overnight so they can complete the exercise, because they've been getting lots of bad marks recently.

What's the difference? In the first, the act of kindness you give doesn't cost you anything (unless you want to argue that five seconds of your time and the effort of talking are extremely valuable!).

In the second example, you are putting your own chances of good marks at risk because you know your friend really needs a break right now. It's going to cost you but you do it anyway.

An amazing example of altruism

In September 1987, a 23-year-old man, Alex Cumba, suffered a seizure while standing at the edge of the platform of a busy subway station in New York, and fell onto the rails, unconscious.

Without hesitation, three other passengers, Melvin Shadd, Edwin Ortiz and Jeff Kuhn, jumped down onto the tracks and rescued Alex from the path of an incoming train.

All four survived.

Melvin Shadd said, "We just had to react."

"YOU CAN ALWAYS, ALWAYS GIVE SOMETHING — EVEN IF IT IS ONLY KINDNESS!"

Anne Frank

Let's get up to date!

Philosophers have argued about ethics for centuries, so let's skip forward and look at two opposite viewpoints.

On the one hand, the German philosopher Friedrich Nietzsche argued that people are naturally EGOTISTIC, which means they think about themselves first and foremost. This is because it's natural which therefore makes it right that we should behave this way.

On the other hand, men like the Swiss philosopher Jean-Jacques Rousseau believed that the human species had been born "good" – and that there had been a time in our past when people were "noble savages", who helped each other, because it was natural to do so. They only started to do bad things because they became corrupted by money, society, etc.

Auguste Comte, the man who brought the word altruism into popular usage, believed that we are born with many obligations – to our predecessors, to our descendants, to our contemporaries.

To live for others, for individual people to serve all of humanity, he argued, made perfect sense, since humanity is, quite simply, people. He also believed that this was the path to a common source of happiness for everyone and therefore that this is good.

However, there's still a problem here. We can argue all we like about whether people are basically good or bad, but we haven't yet defined what we mean by the words "good" or "bad". You might think you know what these words mean, but for philosophers, that's not precise enough. For many philosophers, good and bad are simply how we *feel* about things; not what is actually *true*.

The Scottish philosopher David Hume had something to say about this.

According to Hume, a statement like "murder is wrong" doesn't make sense, because it only begs the question "why?" or "who says it is?" and doesn't actually offer a reason.

On the other hand, things that can be said with real truth are undebatable, such as statements like "cows have four legs".

He took this argument further and said that we can never use logic to create or prove moral laws, as Plato had thought possible.

So how do we know how we should act towards each other? Might it be possible to work it out in some way?

Utilitarianism

In Britain, in the eighteenth and nineteenth centuries, two philosophers, Jeremy Bentham and later John Stuart Mill, thought that it was. They developed an idea that came to be known as UTILITARIANISM.

This is a theory which says the best course of behaviour for society, is one that achieves the most happiness overall. The fundamental principle behind utilitarianism is often summed up as "the greatest good for the greatest number of people" and they wondered if it were possible to make mathematical calculations to actually work this out in any given situation.

How would you do that? With some incredible machine?

Could a modern supercomputer do it? A quantum computer? Still the question remains of who would do the programming – who would decide what the values were, who is worth what, what acts cost what? And so on and so on.

One form of the theory is known as ACT UTILITARIANISM, in which a person is supposed to be unbiased about making the calculations.

So, if you were deciding which one person to throw off a sinking life raft in order that everyone else might live, you should use the same reasoning whether someone you loved were on it, or not. Or even if you yourself were on the raft.

Logically, act utilitarians can get to an altruistic position – it would be right to give your life to save the lives of others, because the death of one person would be outweighed by the survival of many others.

If this sounds familiar, perhaps you're a fan of *Star Trek*, and remember when Spock, about to perform an act of self-sacrifice, explains he's doing it because the needs of a few people, or just one person, are less important than the needs of *many* people.

That's act utilitarianism. Spock probably knew that.

Utilitarianism is interesting to think about, but again, there are problems.

For one thing, in the real world it is probably impossible to work out all of the near-infinite consequences of any action, let alone what their "value" might be. However, even in theory utilitarianism has a problem, in that it still doesn't explain *why* you should be good.

Like other ideas, it just assumes it's good to be good.

Phew! That was a very quick dash through one of the most complicated areas of philosophy, and your head might be spinning now from all this theoretical stuff.

So let's make things a bit more *real* again.

Let's find out what you would do when faced with some everyday dilemmas...

Me before you

Here are four scenarios: which is the odd one out?

1

Your best friend has forgotten their lunch – you give them half of yours so they'll have something to eat at lunchtime and not go hungry. You're not going to get as much lunch as usual but you won't starve.

2

You and your friends all want to go and see the new Pixar movie, but one of you can't go until the following weekend. You all decide to wait so you and all your friends can go together.

3
It's your birthday and you've been given A LOT of sweets by an aunt. Your little brother wants some of the sweets, but you don't give him any – it's your birthday, after all.

4

Your parents are really frazzled by grown-up stuff, so you offer to clear the table after dinner and load the dishwasher so they can go and watch their favourite TV show.

It's not hard to find the odd one out, is it...?

Secret diary...

For the next activity, write down some examples of things you've done that look like numbers 1, 2 or 4, and some examples where you behaved more like number 3. Don't be shy! And don't beat yourself up if you have a few of "number 3" here – none of us are angels; we all do good and bad things, and just for now, it might be interesting to be honest with yourself. You don't have to share this with anyone! It's Top Secret!

Egoism

We met the idea of altruism before – that you should act for the good of others. But there's an opposing idea, that you should act for the good of yourself, and it's called egoism. The people who believe it are called egoists, and the word comes from the Latin *ego* meaning "I".

For an egoist, it's *obvious* that a person has their own best interests at heart. They will therefore do things for their own benefit, regardless of the effect on other people.

Even if they *do* do something that appears to help someone else, it is only because it furthers their own ends too, in some way.

Take an action that appears to be kind or altruistic:

A rich man drops some money into a beggar's cup.

The egoist argues that the rich man only does this to make himself feel better. Perhaps it makes him feel less guilty as he walks past? Or perhaps he does it to show what a nice guy he is to the girl he's walking down the street with? Perhaps he only does it because society has "taught" him to be kind to people less fortunate? Whatever: in some way it makes him feel good, and that's why he does it, not because he really cares for the beggar, or believes it's a moral thing to do.

Either way, the egoist argues that the man only does it for some reason that benefits himself, and that this BENEFIT is GREATER than the actual COST of the money he's given away.

Against Egoism

As we just saw, for an egoist, it's obvious that a person has their own best interests at heart.

Can even this idea be challenged? What is being assumed here?

What's more, believers in egoism might have a hard time explaining certain people's actions, such as rare but incredible examples of people behaving with extraordinary kindness. Remember the men who risked their lives to save Alex Cumba after he fell onto the subway tracks in New York? (page 67) The egoist attempts to argue that it's still serving some self-interested motive, of moral behaviour "learned" from religion, or society, or family.

What then, does the egoist make of a case in which the altruist had a lot of time to consider an action that cost him his life?

Amazing acts of altruism

During the Holocaust, a Polish priest called Maximilian Kolbe volunteered to die in the place of a stranger. Knowing he was going to his death, Kolbe took the place of a man in Auschwitz, so that the man's children would not be deprived of their father.

To explain this, the egoist has to claim that it's because, knowing the priest believes in an afterlife, he is "happy" to die in the father's place, and possibly become a martyr in the process.

In that case, take this one final example.

During the Siege of Leningrad, Hitler's armies surrounded the city for two years, resulting in the starvation of over a million people. Among this extraordinary suffering were a group of scientists who had amassed the world's largest collection of seeds, roots and fruits, to be used as a genetic bank to grow food and so ensure future generations would survive.

This group of nine scientists chose to protect the collection, in order that Russia's food production would be assured in years to come. They starved to death protecting food they could have eaten to live.

"In a world where you can be anything, be kind."

Anonymous

Chapter 4

Are we born kind?

Now it's time to get some more concrete ideas together and focus on the question of whether people are born selfish, as some people believe, or born wanting to help others. For this, it's time for some science, in particular, biology.

You may have had a discussion with your friends or family in which either you, or someone else, said something like this:

"Yes, I know it would be best if we were all nice to each other, but people aren't like that in the real world. In the real world, people are selfish and mean. Life's tough, and you'd better get used to that. You have to protect number one."

Maybe someone followed this up with the old chestnut:

"It's a dog-eat-dog world."

That's an interesting metaphor; one that compares us to animals. It's also a good place to turn to a different discipline, because the egoist might be tempted to argue along these lines: we know that human beings are animals; complicated ones, yes, evolved and smart and so on, but we're all just animals underneath; and so it's stupid to pretend we behave any better than animals do.

But how do animals actually behave? And *are* human beings really just animals?

Well, yes. Or at least, we have been since 1859, and that's a very good point to turn to our next subject... BIOLOGY!

You have probably heard of Charles Darwin, and his theory of evolution, in which he explains how we got here. All of us. Animals too. Plants. The works!

In 1859, he published his book, *On the Origin of Species*, in which he presented one of the most important scientific ideas of ALL TIME. It's easy, the best part of 200 years later, to miss how earth-shattering this book was. At the time, it caused huge controversy, because it overturned the ideas found in the Bible of how human beings were created by God on the sixth day of creation. Instead, it gave an explanation based on the incredibly slow but steady process of EVOLUTION, in which species of all types of life form developed over millions of years, in tiny, tiny steps.

Evolution, Darwin said, rests on a process he called NATURAL SELECTION. Within a species, there are always slight variations between individuals. You're not exactly like your mum or dad, for example, every child is slightly different. You might be tall like your dad, or have blue eyes like your mum. Since such characteristics can be passed down to children (and the offspring of animals too, of course) – we say that the characteristic is HERITABLE, meaning they are inherited.

Actually, the fact that characteristics are heritable had been known for centuries – animal breeders had long used the technique of ARTIFICIAL SELECTION to obtain animals with particular features they wanted to see in the offspring. It's how we have the enormous variety of modern dogs; from poodles to Great Danes, but all descended from the wolf.

It was only a matter of time before someone worked out that the natural world produces selection too. Darwin said that the natural environment had been working its own form of selection upon all forms of life on Earth, literally since life began. So he called it Natural Selection, and it explained where every creature in life had come from. It was the very mechanism by which the earliest forms of life such as single-celled organisms had grown ever more complicated, until we end up with the immense diversity of life on Earth we see today, whether we're talking about bacteria or fungi or sharks or mosses or people.

How does Natural Selection happen?

It's through a mechanism called FITNESS, which works like this: any variation found in an individual of a species may make it either more, or less, "fit" to survive than its other members. So if a gazelle is born to run faster than the other gazelles, it's more likely to survive attacks by cheetahs than its friends.

So if a certain characteristic makes a creature more suited to survive, they are more likely to be able to reproduce. (Unlike the slowest gazelle who got eaten by the cheetah and is now dead, and therefore unable to reproduce.) This characteristic may then be found in its offspring; if so, they will also have greater "fitness". On the other hand, traits that make it less fit will tend to die out from the species, dying with the individuals that were unfortunate enough to have a negative trait.

Hence the phrase "the survival of the fittest" – which is a commonly misunderstood phrase. It doesn't necessarily mean the most athletic or strongest. Here, "fittest" means the individual *most suited* to survive in its environment. In the gazelle example above, it *is* about physical ability. However, "fitness" could mean something very different, such as the brain power to spot patterns in the seasons, which enables you to sow seeds at the right time, grow more food and, as a result, be more likely to survive. It just means you are "fitted" for your environment, in all sorts of ways. Incidentally, it wasn't Darwin who came up with this phrase, but a man called Herbert Spencer who adapted Darwin's theory into other areas, such as the study of society.

Why this long discussion of evolution?!

Well, it's because it has a big role to play in the question of both selfishness and altruism, and we need to understand how it works. That's because despite its ≈simplicity, and its strength, Darwin himself could see it had a problem; a problem he couldn't explain. That problem is; in a word, kindness. Yes, the thing that this whole book is about.

Or, to speak more scientifically, *altruism.*

Now, not all biologists agree (you might have seen by now that it's hard to find universal agreement about anything!), but most of them use the definition of altruism that we saw earlier in the book:

> **Altruism is an act of doing good for someone else in which there is a *cost* to the person doing the good action.**

Now, the way Darwin and his supporters saw his theory of NATURAL SELECTION was like this: life is a struggle, a competition, in effect a kind of warfare between all creatures.

Out of this clash, brutal and uncaring, all species had come to be, including the most exalted and supposedly noble species of all: Humankind. Yet out of this very brutality, the splendour of life had arisen, and not *despite* it, but *because* of it.

Darwin didn't much like this rather bleak conclusion; he felt it was like "confessing a murder", but his belief in his theory compelled him to stick to it.

But is this right? Do we have to agree with Darwin's miserable conclusion?

Maybe not. Other thinkers have seen life differently. One of them was a Russian prince called Peter Kropotkin.

Prince Kropotkin had quite a life; although of royal birth he became a socialist and later a revolutionary anarchist, believing in equality of *all* people, as opposed to rule by the rich or by royalty. Disillusioned with politics, he spent five years travelling, mostly on horseback, across wild parts of the world.

He argued that Darwin's view of nature did not agree with what he had witnessed. Having travelled 50,000 miles, he argued that all around him he had seen examples of cooperation in the animal world. In fact, he said, he had seen just as much cooperation as conflict. Perhaps even more so.

A few of the thousands of examples of cooperation between animals:

Beavers work together to build dams.

Insects form great colonies and work together to build homes to live in.

Vampire bats share blood with individuals who don't succeed in the night's hunt.

So Kropotkin asked – can we find the origin of human goodness in the animal kingdom? However, in Darwinian terms, the problem is this: why would an individual animal ever indulge in *altruistic* behaviour?

According to the theory, any behaviour that puts the animal at greater risk than its non-altruistic equal will, over time, see it fail to compete with that rival, in terms of survival and, therefore, in reproductive success – critically: how likely it is to pass its genes to its descendants.

This means that the genes that made the animal act altruistically in the first place should automatically die out.

In short – altruism should naturally "deselect" itself. But it doesn't. There are examples of altruism, in the very strictest sense, to be found across the animal kingdom – including people.

KINDNESS with a "cost" to the individual being kind, or to use the biological term, ALTRUISM, can be found in many species of animals. From gazelles that put themselves in danger by leaping in the air to warn of an approaching predator, to chimpanzees that adopt babies who have become orphans, to ants that literally turn themselves into food for other ants to eat, the animal kingdom has no shortage of acts of kindness that Darwin's theory seemed to struggle to explain.

Even so, Darwinism is still accepted as the correct theory that explains evolution, so how did this problem get solved?

For that, we need to understand a little about what happened to biology in the twentieth century, and that's all about GENETICS.

Genetics

Genetics is the branch of biology that studies how traits get passed on to our offspring, through our genes, our DNA. It's vital to explaining what happened next, because Charles Darwin knew there was a problem with his own theory – if every individual animal (or human, for that matter) is only looking out for themselves, how could the act of self-sacrifice ever be "selected"? He was particularly bothered by the so-called "social insects". In every hive of bees, for example, there are certain types who are sterile – that means they are unable to reproduce. Instead, they work for the benefit of the queen, so that she may prosper and have lots of offspring. Which is great for the bees as a group. But if every individual is only looking out for itself, as Darwin thought, how could the trait of being sterile ever have evolved by natural selection? By definition, a sterile individual cannot pass on any traits at all, never mind the trait of being sterile. So how could a trait like kindness, like altruism, ever have arisen?

What's the solution?

It's a little complicated, but it's worth understanding.

Although it had been known since the nineteenth century that there had to be something that was being passed from parent to child in order for inheritance to work, it wasn't until the discovery of DNA in the twentieth century that scientists were able to explain exactly how this inheritance worked. DNA is a molecule that contains various genes – the individual sections that provide the "code" that give an organism all its qualities; in the case of people, for example, eye colour, hair colour, blood type, the risk of certain diseases and so on.

Think again about the principle of natural selection. Genes are passed from parents to their children, but since children receive a mixture of genes from mother and father, their children are not the same as they are. Not exactly. These variations are what natural selection then works on, "weeding out" bad variations and reinforcing good ones. By "good" we mean a gene that is beneficial to the individual, which will tend to grow within a species with each succeeding generation because it gives a reproductive advantage to its owner. On the other hand, a gene that is unfavourable to the individual will not be selected for, it will be weeded out. We say it is "deselected".

Now let's suppose there was a new, rare genetic mutation that caused the individual to act in a way that increased the chances of survival of its relatives, *even though it lowered its own chances.* Since relatives have a chance of carrying the same rare gene, this altruism gene could live on in these relatives. It could grow in frequency in the population of the species as a whole, despite the fact that from time to time an individual carrier of the gene will give its life through its altruistic behaviour.

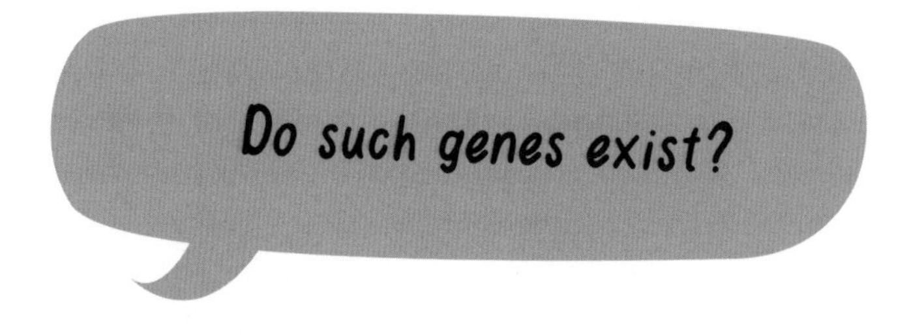

Unquestionably. They are one of the things that define human beings.

That such genes exist is obvious, perhaps too obvious and therefore often overlooked. Looking at higher animals, mammals and so on, in almost every species the offspring are nurtured for some time by one or both parents until they can stand on their own two, or four feet. They do this at considerable cost to themselves. In the case of people, human babies are so helpless that they require nurturing for several years before they can provide for themselves; at great cost to the parent. This is because parents are altruistic towards their children; without it, the human species would not exist.

Kin selection

Kin selection is the solution to Darwin's problem of how a trait that might be bad for an individual's chances of survival could nonetheless grow within a population of animals. It's a concept that is easily misunderstood (even in university level textbooks about the subject!). It's *not* the idea that individuals do good towards people they are related to, i.e., with whom they share lots of genes. Instead, it's the simple idea that a gene that is potentially harmful to an individual can nevertheless thrive in the population as a whole. And that gene could be a gene for altruism, for example.

It's important to note that these ideas are not just theoretical – they have been measured directly in studies of animals such as red squirrels and sun-tailed monkeys. It's even been demonstrated in plants!

For example, it's been shown that certain trees can distinguish roots belonging to their "relatives" as opposed to other trees. Furthermore, they can even send nutrients to their kin if they sense they are struggling. They can, for instance, distribute carbon, from individuals with a lot of it, to those with less. Even more amazingly, they do this using the branching, threadlike networks of the mycelia of fungi that spread underground in the soil of the forest, connecting the trees.

Does this mean that if you have altruistic parents, you will be altruistic too? And if not, you won't?

Genetic inheritance is not that simple. For one thing, other factors can affect how altruistic you are. One piece of research has shown that genetic tendencies may account for 30–60 per cent of altruistic behaviours; another study that altruism is 50 per cent inherited. That means there's plenty of room for a range of other factors that come into play. What sort of other factors? Well, as an example, if we look at another human characteristic, average lifespan, it's not just a question of how long your parents live for. Their genetics will of course play a big part, but so do many other things, such as what you eat throughout your lifetime, how stressed you are, where you live and even how wealthy you are! Just this week, as I write this book, it's been announced that men in Chelsea, London, live 27 *years longer* than men in Blackpool as a result of such factors.

Before we finish talking about genetics, we need to discuss one more biologist, a man called Richard Dawkins, and his highly influential book, *The Selfish Gene*.

Ask anyone who knows this book by its title, but who hasn't actually read it, and they'll almost certainly tell you that it's about how our genes make us selfish. That's unfortunate, because not only do we often judge books by their covers, we also sometimes judge them by their titles. What the title of this book seems to tell us is in fact *the complete opposite* of what the book actually says. Dawkins himself admitted, many years after the book first appeared, that he regretted his choice of title. Here's why.

Dawkins used Darwin's position as a starting point, but introduced one big idea that he argues makes sense of all the disputes and disagreements surrounding evolution, and explains why behaviour that might appear illogical arises.

The idea is this: that it is not in fact the *individual animal* that natural selection works on, but their *individual genes.*

It is the gene that is "selfish" – its only goal is to make more copies of itself.

When the book was published, it upset a lot of people. To many, it seemed to present a very miserable view of the world. Much like Darwin feeling his theory was like confessing to a murder, some people thought that Dawkins meant that we humans are just brainless vehicles being controlled by nothing more than the survival instinct of our genes.

This might *at first* seem depressing – where is the room here for things we feel are good: things like love, and friendship? Like kindness?

Pause to consider this though; we know these good things do exist – we see them every day, all around us, everywhere in the world. If we accept the theory of evolution and of natural selection as true, and if it's true that it is the gene itself that is the base of these things, then we come to one startling conclusion: what it means is this – that altruism exists not *despite* selfishness, but actually *because* of it.

It is the selfish behaviour of *genes* that has given rise to the altruistic behaviour of *individuals*. This is what Dawkins' book, *The Selfish Gene*, actually tells us.

Is that depressing? I don't think it is. It's actually *very* positive, because what it suggests is that ultimately the key to survival must be through altruism, because even "selfishness" itself has recognized that cooperation and kindness is the best way forward.

That's an extraordinary thought – in the end, selfishness has been defeated. It has recognized that kindness and cooperation are the only way to survive.

"What you do
makes a difference,

and you have
to decide

what kind of
difference you
want to make."

Jane Goodall, biologist

Chapter 5

Kindness and you

We have taken a quick look at kindness. Where it came from, and some of the main ideas around it. But what about ourselves? What can we do? How should we go forward in the world?

Small steps to change the world with kindness

It's good to be kind, and it benefits not just others, but ourselves too – the kinder we are to others, the easier and happier we feel about ourselves.

Here are a few simple things you can do every day:

- ★ **Tell people that you like them. That you're happy they are there. That they mean something to you. It costs you nothing and yet you can really make someone's day.**

- ★ **Be a good listener. Many people don't feel heard – you can do something great for someone else by just listening to them, properly. Listen to their fears, their worries, their hopes, their dreams.**

- ★ **Help those who are less fortunate than you.**

- ★ **Help those who are *more* fortunate than you.**

- ★ **Think first! One thing we can all do is to think before we act on impulse. Sometimes our first reaction to a difficult situation can make things worse – someone is mean to us, we say something unkind back, and it spirals out of control. So take a breath. Drop your shoulders. Count to ten!**

- ★ **Whenever you hear about a difficult situation, try to see things from both sides. If you hear about an argument, try to practise being "in the shoes" of the people on either side. Maybe you immediately think one side is right and the other is wrong, but just as an experiment, try to see why the other side feel the way they do. Remember, it's very easy to see a lot of things as facts, when really they are just opinions.**

What do you think? Can you add in some more simple things you can do every day to make the world a better place?

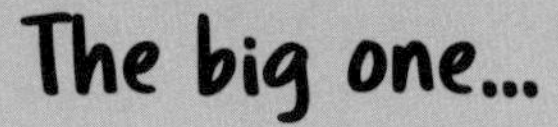

Be kind to yourself

If you cannot be kind to yourself, you will have real trouble being kind to anyone else, in the long run. If you believe you are kind, you will see more kindness in the world around you.

What kind things can you do for yourself?

It could be something like listening to your favourite songs, making a den to read in or have some chill-out time. It doesn't matter how small it is – just make being kind to yourself and others an active part of your daily life. You can do more than one thing if you want! Just see what happens as you include more kindness into your life.

Add some ideas here for what you can do today to be kind to yourself.

Keep a diary

You might decide to keep a diary in which you write down your thoughts and actions each day. If you have done something unkind, be honest with yourself. You don't need to be hard on yourself, or judge yourself, here. This diary is just for you. Writing things down is a really powerful way of getting things out of your head and seeing them more clearly. As you keep the journal, you might also see that being kind every day is infectious – not only do you want to do more of it, you might start to see it spreading around you.

If nothing else, if you start noticing when other people are kind, it can change your view of the world – you can see it as a kinder place than you might be tempted to see it as if you only watched the evening news...

Good news vs bad news

Have a think about the stories we expose ourselves to: the news is a perfect example – if you watch or read the news, it's very easy to conclude the world is just an awful place.

Imagine you were an alien species come to observe Earth and all you saw was the TV news?! You'd very quickly be jumping back into your spaceship and hitting the lightspeed button. This is because the people who make the news know that we are more attracted to bad news than good news. This might sound crazy when you first think about it, but the news is a product to be sold like anything else. The people who make it want you to keep coming back for more, almost like an addiction, even if that addiction is bad for you.

Psychologists say that it takes five pieces of good news to have the same "importance" in the brain as one piece of bad news. It's probably another evolutionary thing, to make sure we look out for potential danger, but the result in the modern busy world is that it's all too easy to conclude that people are terrible and the planet is a mess.

Take a look around you, keep that diary, and just begin to notice that *most* of the time, *most* people are helpful, generous, kind and so on. It just doesn't make the six o'clock news...

We are really only beginning to understand the effects of the internet on the human brain. It is clear that it is a powerful thing, and it is neither "good" nor "bad" in itself, but the things it can do can certainly be either of those.

When it comes to social media specifically, it's worth knowing that some of the very people who write the code for platforms like Facebook and Twitter or who work for Google or Apple, have admitted that they use techniques to make people addicted to using them (if you don't believe me, google it!). They studied how people become addicted to gambling (which seems to be to do with the random nature of winning from time to time amidst a lot of losing), and applied the same methods to their apps.

All those little icons; the likes, the hearts, and so on, have been shown to have a powerful addictive effect by triggering the brain's "reward" centres, just as gambling does.

So that's the first thing to know about social media – you might end up using it more than you thought you would. Or actually even want to. Have you ever put your device down, but two minutes later you find it's in your hand again, and you're checking social media? And you didn't even realize you had picked it up again? If you catch yourself doing this, you might want to think about activating time limits to warn you when you've spent too long checking your status. Even if you don't have your own device yet, or don't use social media very much, it's hard to escape and ignore as you get older. It's never too early to learn the positives and negatives to social media.

WARNING! Social media can make you mean and miserable

The second thing to know about social media is this – it can be bad for your mental health. True, the use of social media can make you feel connected, and find friends, especially if you're someone who is a bit "different" for some reason, is shy, for example, or has a hard time making friends at school, etc. And that's great as far as it goes, but the problem is that study after study has shown that the use of social media can do two bad things. First, it can make you miserable. And second, it can make you meaner.

This seems to be because of the anonymity of the internet. You are not face to face with the person you're interacting with on Twitter, or Facebook. You may not even be using your real name; if you're on Roblox, you definitely aren't – you don't even provide an email address. That seems to make it far easier for people to say all sorts of mean things and when they do that, you are far more likely to respond with something unkind in return.

The funny thing about "social media" is that there is a lot of evidence to show it is actually making us all more "anti-social".

So be careful when you use it, how long you use it for each day, and how you interact with people.

Experiencing unkindness and cyberbullying online

If you are on the receiving end of unkindness online, don't keep it to yourself. Talk to a grown-up you trust and seek their help and advice. If you can, block the person (or people) leaving the hurtful comments and report them to the app provider if you need to. If you can't block them, distance yourself from the online platforms in question and consider deleting your profile while you recover from the bullying. Don't suffer in silence, ever. (See also page 125 for more ways to deal with unkindness that is directed at you.)

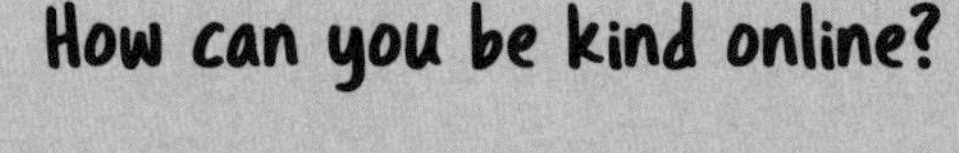

How can you be kind online?

Be kind to you

Install apps or activate alerts to warn you when you have spent too long on your phone, tablet or computer.

Be kind to others

Remember the golden rule - do unto others etc. and if you like, add in a new golden rule: if you wouldn't say something to someone's face, don't post it on their feed.

Add your ideas here – maybe even make a poster!

"A KINDNESS IS NEVER WASTED."

Aesop, *The Lion and the Mouse*

What do you do when people are unkind to you?

This can be tricky and upsetting and cause you to feel all kinds of uncomfortable emotions. So what do you do in the moment? Here are some tips to help:

- **Try not to react in the moment. Stay calm.**
- **Maybe remove yourself from the situation if you can, so you can think about it slowly.**
- **If you can't get out of the situation, try to answer the other person with respect. Again, try to stay calm (did I say that already!?). Pretend if you have to! Not only will this make you feel more in control, you will show the unkind person's actions more clearly for what they are.**
- **Don't stoke the fire. You will handle things much better if you give yourself time to think.**
- **Ask yourself some questions: Why are they behaving like this? What is their motive? Have you misunderstood each other? Did *you* do something mean to *them*?**

This is where empathy comes into play – something we talked about earlier where you imagine yourself in someone else's shoes: Don't assume you know what other people are going through.

Try to find out more about what other people think, even when you disagree with them.

Don't assume that because your parents or another grown-up told you something, you have to think the same way. You can be the change! For example, you might think it's good to recycle but your parents can't be bothered. You can still do your bit and you can hold onto your principles. One day, you will have children of your own perhaps, and your own house, and you can be as green as you like. Remember that you are the future!

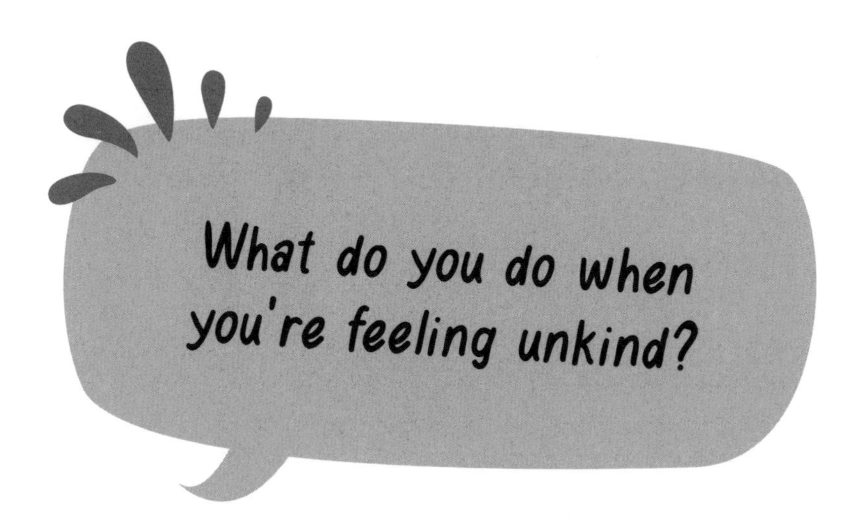

There's going to be times when people will make you want to SCREAM!

- ★ **Take a deep breath, try to see how your body is feeling. Are you tense? Feeling all chewed up? Where is that coming from?**
- ★ **Is it *worth* being mean? You might really feel you want to now, but what will happen if you do? Will you lose a friend over it? Is it worth it?**
- ★ **Try to see what's motivating you. Why do you feel unkind? Are your feelings in proportion to the reality of the situation?**
- ★ **Is there something else you can do instead of being mean? Would it be an idea to let things drop for now and see how you feel later?**

Think back to a time you when were mean to someone, and what the result of this was.

Now think of a time when you were kind or generous, *even when you didn't feel like it*, and what the result was...

See the difference?

Of course, it can take a little effort sometimes to be kind in the face of difficult things, but in the long run, it can make life *much* easier. It's worth the effort.

"There are two ways of spreading light:

to be the candle

or the mirror that reflects it."

Edith Wharton

Chapter 6

You can change the world!

Yes, you can! Trust me. Some people feel that it's pointless doing things to try to make the world better. They point at all the big bad things that are going on and say, "What can I do? It makes no difference if I decide to recycle when all the big petrol companies are still drilling for oil. It makes no difference if I'm kind to people, when so many people are selfish." But this simply isn't true.

For one thing; if you decide to do your best to be kind to other people, or to be kind to the planet, then the world *has* changed – there is one more person in it doing things well. The world is already a little bit better.

"So what?" you might say. "One more person, big deal!" But actually, sometimes all it takes is one person.

Be the change!

Remember the title of the series this book is part of? *Be the Change!* That title comes from a famous quote that goes like this: "Be the change you wish to see in the world". What this means is, you don't need to go around trying to convince other people to be better, just be better yourself. You are the only person you have control over, so just live in the way you think everyone should live, and if you do, you might start to inspire people around you to live differently too. But you don't need to worry about that – just be the change you wish to see in the world. If that's by being kind, then be kind. If that's by being "green", then be green.

You still might wonder how this helps, since you're only one person. However, if you think about it, ALL CHANGE starts with one person. *Someone* has to be the first to think something new or do something new.

People often say that "Be the change you wish to see in the world" was first said by an Indian man called Mahatma Gandhi. In fact, as often with famous quotes, what he actually said was slightly different. He said: "We but mirror the world. If we could change ourselves, the tendencies in the world would also change." This idea has been simplified over the years to the "be the change" version, but Gandhi was right.

Gandhi is a great example of how one person can make a huge difference. What he is best known for is this: India was once ruled by Britain, a country halfway around the world. Gandhi thought this was wrong, and his actions, beliefs and protests started a movement that inspired a whole country to rise up and fight for their independence from rule by a foreign power! Sometimes, one person can truly change the world.

"Never doubt that a small group of thoughtful, committed citizens can change the world. Indeed, it is the only thing that ever has."

Margaret Mead

The book is nearly finished. You've read a lot about kindness. Has anything changed for you?

Do you feel differently about the subject now than you did before?

Do you feel differently about yourself now?

Do any of these apply to you (maybe more than one)? [Circle the statements that get a thumbs up!]

- **I'm going to try to be kinder now.**
- **I still don't see the point; I'm going to look out for "number one", i.e. me!**
- **I see that I am kinder than I thought I was.**
- **I see that other people are kinder than I thought they were.**
- **I can see how kindness is like a "ripple effect" - one act of kindness can cause another, which causes another, and so on...**
- **I see that I can "be the change"; even if it's just me who's kinder from now on, the world is still better than it was yesterday.**

If you're feeling good about kindness now, that's great!

If you're still to be convinced, I hope you will at least keep thinking about it, looking out for it in your daily life, experimenting with it. It really is a happier way to live being kind than being mean!

... how is it that sometimes people can do really bad things to others?

Even if you're not actively unkind, how is it that we can walk past a homeless person, someone living on the street, begging for money? Many of us can and do just walk past them. We tell ourselves stories such as, "If I gave them money, they'd only spend it on drugs," when we have no idea if that's true. If it was your Auntie Doris sitting there, you'd immediately help her.

Psychologists have discovered that, in our minds, we divide people into "in-groups" and "out-groups". For example, you put your friends and your family into your in-group, but you tend to put strangers, people you've never met, people you see on the news, etc. into your out-group.

Some people have very small in-groups, maybe just their immediate family. The smallest possible would be just you! Others include all sorts of people – even people they don't know; for example, they give money to help people starving on the other side of the world because they care even for these people they will never meet.

In-groups and out-groups can change, shift and overlap. For example, if you're a football fan, your in-group might include City players when you're watching an England match, but when it comes to the local derby with United, suddenly you're at war again. Or, have you ever noticed in those films where aliens invade Earth, we all stop squabbling and team up against the invaders? That's because we've suddenly put *everyone* in our in-group. (Everyone apart from the aliens...)

This idea is very powerful, and actually quite scary, because experiments have shown that when you regard someone as being in your out-group, your brain reacts differently to them – in fact, you *literally think of them as being less than human.* Using brain scans, this has been shown to be the case. This is quite a terrifying and very important thing to know. It's how certain terrible things in history have been able to happen, the Holocaust, for example – because one group of people were literally seeing another group not just as different, *but as less than human.*

Of course, it's here that we understand how people can be racist, homophobic or sexist. You and I might find it very hard to understand how people can be any of these things, but according to psychologists, it's because the brain of a racist person literally interprets a Black person as being inferior.

So how can we change this?

It's really important that we learn about people who are different from us. It's far too easy to take the world as it is and think that's how it has always been, or how it should be. This is why we have things like Black History Month, to try to educate everyone as to why and how inequality between black and white people came into being, why it still exists and what we can do about it.

The main thing we can do, as before, is learn to see things from someone else's point of view.

That's why READING is so important. Scientists have now proven what writers like me have known for years – that when you read about someone else, you *become* them in a certain way. You empathize with them, you feel their pains and their joys as if they were your own.

Books can be *really* powerful – it's said that the book *Uncle Tom's Cabin*, published in 1852 by Harriet Beecher Stowe, had a huge effect on public opinion about the slave trade, in fact that it helped lay the groundwork for the American Civil War, which was largely fought over that issue.

Likewise, the book *Black Beauty* by Anna Sewell, played a huge role in the improvement of the treatment of animals, because the book showed how cruel people were being to horses. The book is written from the horse's point of view, and if a book can even make us empathize with a different species, you can see how powerful this process is!

So read, read, read, and encourage others to do the same.

Eco-altruism – save the world with kindness

Here's a new idea: maybe the most important form of kindness at this point in history. Maybe the people that we most need to be kind towards haven't even been born yet. The climate crisis threatens our lives, but it threatens the lives of future generations even more.

Therefore, perhaps this is the group of people we need to show the greatest kindness to right now, to protect their very lives. How do we do this? We can do this by doing as much as we can, both individually and collectively, to reduce carbon emissions. We can take individual action on this, and we can also try to convince other people of the importance of this. We can choose not to buy things from companies that are not doing enough to prevent climate change, which is a very powerful thing, because companies take notice if they are losing money.

So there is reason for hope and there are things we can all do, and the future should see a rise in what we might call "eco-altruism" – it's simply kindness towards those yet to come.

Final thoughts: the courage to be kind

It can seem like it takes courage to be kind. Many people do not do kind things because they are afraid. Because they have been let down in the past, because something bad once happened to them, and they have decided to protect themselves as a result, for the rest of their lives.

They don't act with kindness; they live with fear.

This book argues that kindness is the answer to that fear.

That every act of kindness you do, no matter how small, makes the world a better place. That kindness spreads. That love is like an infection; just as a disease can spread and be bad, so love can spread and bring goodness and healing. And change.

That everything that changed for the better in this world started with just one person.

That YOU
can be
the change.

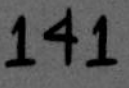

About the Author

Marcus Sedgwick is an internationally award-winning author of novels for adults, teenagers, and younger children, of non-fiction, graphic novels, academic papers and even the odd picture book. Perhaps best known for *Midwinterblood*, which won the Printz Award, America's most notable prize for writing for young adults, alongside *Revolver* and *The Ghosts of Heaven*, both of which achieved Printz Honor status. He has taught creative writing for fifteen years, at Arvon, Ty Newydd and elsewhere, and was for three years Author-in-Residence at Bath Spa University. He has written articles for numerous national newspapers and magazines, and currently lives in the south of France.

About the Illustrator

Thomas Taylor's first professional commission after leaving art school was the cover art for *Harry Potter and the Philosopher's Stone* by J. K. Rowling. He then went on to illustrate, and also write, more than a dozen picture books (most notably the Clovis the Tiger books) before venturing into the world of children's fiction himself. His bestselling middle grade novel *Malamander* (2019) has been translated into 20 languages, and introduces a five-book series about a mysterious seaside town called Eerie-on-Sea. Thomas currently lives on the south coast of England.

Be The Change: Be Calm

Rise Up and Don't Let Anxiety Hold You Back

Marcus Sedgwick

978-1-80007-412-5

£10.99

You can conquer your worries. The power is within you!

We all experience anxiety from time to time. It can feel overwhelming and uncomfortable, and stops us from doing the things we enjoy – so what on earth can we do about it?

Be the Change: Be Calm will show you how to shut down anxiety with fun and simple ways to calm your mind by listening to what your body is telling you. Ever tried the half-salamander exercise? You should! And have you ever performed a body scan? Thought not. These amazing activities along with many others will become your toolkit to a calmer and happier life.

Award-winning author Marcus Sedgwick takes us on a fascinating journey to find out where anxiety comes from, looking at the power of storytelling in terms of training our brain to overcome worries. He also shows us what animals can teach us about dealing with stress AND introduces us to our second brain! Hello! It's time to make CALM your superpower.

ARE YOU READY TO BE KIND TO YOUR MIND?

Have you enjoyed this book?
If so, why not write a review on your favourite website?

If you're interested in finding out more about our books,
Find us on Facebook at **Summersdale Publishers**, on
Twitter at **@Summersdale** and on Instagram
at **@summersdalebooks** and get in touch.
We'd love to hear from you!

Thanks very much for buying this Summersdale book.

www.summersdale.com

Additional image credits:

pp.7, 31 – pen and line © Mark Rademaker/Shutterstock.com; p.8 and throughout – stars © Alona Savchuk/Shutterstock.com; p.10 and throughout – stationery © rangsan paidaen/Shutterstock.com; p.11 – heart and hands © Maarina Vlasova/Shutterstock.com; p.19 – trolley © Tiwa K/Shutterstock.com; p.29 – question marks/Shutterstock.com; p.34 – hands and hearts © Tetiana Yurchenko/Shutterstock.com; pp.39, 47 – quill pen © Ramosh artworks/Shutterstock.com; p.49 – talking heads © Paul Craft/Shutterstock.com; p.58 – lightbulbs © Receh Lancar Jaya/Shutterstock.com; p.63 – decision making © Stmool/Shutterstock.com; p.70 – signpost © Gaba Duran/Shutterstock.com; p.75 – icons © Freud/Shutterstock.com; p.83 – hand and heart © Tetiana Yurchenko/Shutterstock.com; p.89 – zebra and elephant © Vilmos Varga/Shutterstock.com; p.101 – double helix © primiaou/Shutterstock.com; p.120 and throughout – phone and thumbs up/thumbs down © Freud/Shutterstock.com; p.126 – characters with question marks © Sapunkele/Shutterstock.com; p.132 – hands © Tasha Art/Shutterstock.com